True Friends

by Sharon Franklin
illustrated by Tony Sansevero

Scott Foresman
is an imprint of

Glenview, Illinois • Boston, Massachusetts • Mesa, Arizona
Shoreview, Minnesota • Upper Saddle River, New Jersey

Every effort has been made to secure permission and provide appropriate credit for photographic material. The publisher deeply regrets any omission and pledges to correct errors called to its attention in subsequent editions.

Unless otherwise acknowledged, all photographs are the property of Pearson.

Photo locations denoted as follows: Top (T), Center (C), Bottom (B), Left (L), Right (R), Background (Bkgd)

Illustrations by Tony Sansevero

Photograph 24 ©Bettman/Corbis

ISBN 13: 978-0-328-39423-4
ISBN 10: 0-328-39423-8

1 2 3 4 5 6 7 8 9 10 V0G1 17 16 15 14 13 12 11 10 09 08

"Fifty-one dollars, fifty-two dollars, $53.75." Zoe, the chorus treasurer, looked up with a grin. "Our in-school bake sale today was a huge success! Thank you all for your help at lunch time!"

Tabitha looked around the school's music room as everyone cheered. She was cheering too, so no one would suspect anything, but inside she felt sick. She was the only one who knew that there should be $55.75 in the money box.

The school chorus had held two bake sales and three car washes to earn travel money for its spring performance. The Song Makers had been invited for the second year in a row to perform along with the middle-school chorus at the state capital in Salem, Oregon.

"Tabitha? Oh, Tabitha? Are you even on this planet?"

Tabitha looked up to see Zoe frantically waving her hands at her.

"Isn't it great, Tabitha?" Zoe asked. "We need to have only one more bake sale. Then we'll have enough money to go to Salem for sure. Do you want to come over? My mom's going to pick me up in a couple of minutes."

Tabitha smiled. "I can't, Zoe. I promised my little brother, Kwame, that I'd help him learn to ride his new bike today."

Zoe squished up her face and said, "Yeah, brothers!" Then she waved and hurried out the door.

Tabitha went out the door after Zoe. As she walked home she remembered what a high point singing at the capital had been for the chorus last year. Now, with the money from their bake sales and car washes, they would be able to go again.

But Tabitha had seen something that made it hard for her to share in her friends' excitement. In her mind she replayed what she had seen earlier from outside the music room.

Tabitha's friend Abbey had been the first to arrive for chorus practice, and she was alone in the room. From the hallway Tabitha saw Abbey open the money box on the table. Tabitha watched her take out a dollar, and then another, and stuff them both into her pocket.

When she arrived home, Tabitha could hear Bounce scratching at the door. "Bounce, no! No scratching!"

When she finally got in through the door, Bounce was wriggling with excitement. Tabitha picked up her beagle puppy and snuggled against his soft fur. "What would you do, Bounce?" she asked. "Should I tell everyone what Abbey did? It would be awful to ruin everyone's good mood and make them angry at Abbey, but what she did was wrong!"

Bounce whined and licked her face in response. "Some help you are, my friend!" Tabitha said, smiling at Bounce while she dangled a toy in front of his nose.

That night at dinner, Tabitha pushed the food around on her plate.

"Tabitha," her mom said. "Don't play with your food. What's the matter? Are you sick?"

"No, Mom. Maybe I'm just tired. May I be excused?"

Tabitha walked slowly up the stairs to her room to start her homework. But she couldn't concentrate because what she had seen kept bothering her.

"Why would Abbey do something like that?" she asked herself. "But why am I even asking why she did it? It was just plain wrong!"

There was a soft knock on her door.

"Tabitha, it's Mom. May I come in?"

"Sure, Mom," Tabitha answered.

Tabitha's mom came in and sat on the bed. "Tabitha, what is it?" she asked. "I know something's wrong."

"It's nothing," Tabitha replied glumly.

"Maybe it's a problem at school?" Mom asked gently.

"Oh, Mom. I don't know what to do," Tabitha said at last, as a tear rolled down her cheek. Before she knew it, Tabitha had told her mom the whole story of seeing Abbey take the money.

Her mom listened quietly. Then she sighed and smiled. "Well, Tabitha," she said. "It's true that what Abbey did is wrong. Do you have any idea why she may have done it?"

"No," Tabitha sniffled, "but I know it's wrong. I should tell the other kids."

"You're right," her mom replied. "But have you thought about talking with Abbey first?"

"I'm afraid to," said Tabitha.

"It won't be easy, but it's important to learn that things may not always be cut and dried," Tabitha's mom said.

"Cut and dried?" Tabitha asked.

"I'm not saying that it's all right to steal," Tabitha's mom explained, "but Abbey might have stolen the money for a reason that you don't know about. People often concentrate so much on *what* happened that they never think to ask *why* it happened."

Tabitha was very quiet for a moment. Then she said, "Well, even if Bounce were starving, I wouldn't steal! Maybe I would see if I could rake someone's leaves to earn money to feed him."

"That is a great solution," Tabitha's mom replied, "but Abbey wasn't thinking as clearly as you are. Maybe talking about it with her will help Abbey think of solutions."

Tabitha felt more confident now. Tomorrow, she decided, she would talk to Abbey.

"OK, honey," her mom said. "Finish up your homework, brush your teeth, and hop into bed." She smiled at Tabitha and leaned over and kissed her on the cheek.

The next afternoon, Tabitha sat in class and watched the clock. She waited for school to be over for the week. She was nervous about talking to Abbey, but she was anxious to get it over with. When the bell finally rang, Tabitha jumped up and was the first person out the door. She hurried down to Abbey's classroom.

When Tabitha saw Abbey come out, she smiled at her and motioned for her to come over. "Hi, Abbey," she said. "Would you like to walk home together?"

"Sure," Abbey agreed.

Tabitha had practiced what she wanted to say. She waited until they were away from the other kids, and then she took a deep breath.

"I saw you take the money, Abbey," she said.

Abbey stopped walking and looked down at the ground. Tabitha didn't know what to say or do next.

Finally, Abbey breathed a long sigh, and Tabitha could see that she was crying.

"Are you going to tell on me?" Abbey asked. "I feel terrible, and I want to give the money back, but I'm too afraid."

"But Abbey," Tabitha said, "why did you take it?"

"My dad lost his job," Abbey sobbed. "We don't have the money to pay for the chorus shirt that I need for the concert in Salem."

Tabitha was shocked, saddened, and relieved all at the same time. There had been a reason that Abbey took the money! Stealing had not been the right thing to do, but at least Abbey hadn't taken the money out of greed.

Tabitha was surprised to find herself smiling. Abbey looked at her, and she did not understand Tabitha's smile. "This is serious, Tabitha. There's nothing to smile about. I did a terrible thing."

Then Tabitha thought about why she was smiling. "I'm smiling because I'm relieved," she said. "I understand, Abbey. I truly understand! And so will everyone else. I just know they will. We need you in the chorus. We can't go to Salem without you. We can make this right."

Abbey cried, "What should I do? Everyone will hate me. Can't I just put the money back without telling anyone?"

"No, I don't think you can," Tabitha replied. "If you don't take responsibility, people will wonder where the extra money came from."

"I'll just drop out of the chorus. No one needs to know anything. Everyone will hate me if I tell the truth. No one will understand."

"You're wrong," Tabitha said. "I understand, and I'll help you. We'll tell them together."

Abbey had stopped crying. She looked up, smiled, and nodded her head in agreement with what Tabitha had said.

Tabitha and Abbey arranged to meet on Saturday at Tabitha's house before the last bake sale. Tabitha was ready exactly on time, but Abbey was late.

Tabitha bit her lower lip. *What if she decides not to come?* Tabitha thought to herself. *Then what will I do? Will I have to tell everyone myself?*

Just at the moment Tabitha decided to go on ahead to the bake sale, she saw Abbey coming down the street. She was holding a huge box out in front of her.

"I'm sorry that I'm late," Abbey said when she reached the corner. "The cookies just came out of the oven."

Tabitha gave a sigh of relief and grinned at Abbey. The two girls set off down the street toward their school.

By the time they arrived at the bake sale, a line had already formed to buy cookies and muffins. Everyone in the community wanted to help the chorus raise enough money to go to Salem, and the bake sale gave people a good excuse to eat some cookies and muffins!

Zoe had been at the bake sale for a while before Tabitha and Abbey arrived. She gave Tabitha and Abbey high-fives after they had set their boxes of cookies down on the table.

"Mmmm," Zoe said as she smelled Abbey's cookies. "Let's get these cookies out. Everyone knows that Abbey's cookies always sell the best!"

Abbey gave Tabitha a nervous smile and opened her box of cookies.

Zoe was managing the money box, and she flipped it open after Tabitha and Abbey had set out their cookies.

"Hey, look! We've already earned nine dollars!" Zoe pointed out to the two girls.

Tabitha steered Abbey down to the other end of the table. She leaned close to her and said, "Abbey, stop acting so nervous. People are going to think there's something wrong."

"That's because there is!" Abbey replied. "After all, I stole our money last week. How would you feel if you knew that in a few hours all your friends were going to hate you?"

"Abbey," Tabitha whispered. "They're not going to hate you. Trust me."

After the sale, everyone gathered for a final count of their earnings. "That's $53.00, $54.00, $55.75!" Zoe exclaimed. "With the $260.00 that we've already put into the bank, that makes $315.75! We're $15.75 over our goal!"

The members of the Song Makers chorus erupted into cheers while Abbey and Tabitha stood silently and watched.

They both knew that it was time to say something. The two girls moved toward Zoe and the money box. In a loud, clear voice, Tabitha announced, "Actually, we are $17.75 over our goal."

Slowly, the group became quiet. Zoe, looking puzzled, asked, "What do you mean, Tabitha?

Tabitha looked at Abbey, and Abbey nervously pulled the two dollars from her pocket. "I took this from the money box on Thursday before chorus practice. Zoe left the room for a moment, and she trusted me to watch the money box. I'm very sorry."

Everyone remained quiet. No one knew what to say. Their faces showed surprise and disbelief. Finally, Zoe took the money from Abbey and put it into the box. "Why did you do it, Abbey?" she asked.

Abbey held her breath and tried not to cry. She had a difficult time speaking, and all she could manage were squeaks.

Everyone turned to Tabitha. Tabitha put her arm around Abbey's shoulder, took a deep breath, and told them everything.

When she finished, they all crowded around Abbey and tried to cheer her up.

"Abbey, why didn't you tell us about your dad? I know the feeling. It happened to my dad," one Song Maker said.

"Abbey, you could have borrowed my shirt from last year. It would fit you," said another.

"Abbey, I have some extra money saved. I would have loaned you some," said Zoe.

As the circle of friends gathered around Abbey, Tabitha smiled with relief.

Now Zoe was rapping on the table with a pencil. "Quiet, everyone. Quiet! I'm your treasurer, and we need to make some decisions."

As the questions and chatter died down, Zoe continued.

"Let's all thank Abbey. She's brave. She did something wrong, but she admitted her mistake."

Abbey breathed deeply and said, "Thank you. I've learned my lesson. I know now to talk to my friends if I have a problem. I want you all to know that I felt horrible after I took our money."

"It's all right, Abbey!" they replied.

Tears were running down Abbey's cheeks, but she had a big smile on her face too.

Zoe rapped her pencil again. "OK, everyone, let's take a vote. How many of you would like to use the extra money to buy Abbey's chorus shirt?"

All the hands shot up immediately. Everyone was in favor of the idea.

"And how many vote that we head into the cafeteria to share the good news with our parents?" Zoe asked.

This time, their hands were raised even higher. They were ready to celebrate their upcoming trip. The Song Makers' meeting ended as the chorus filed into their school cafeteria singing, "Hi ho, hi ho! It's off to Salem we go!"

A Family Chorus

Many years ago, a family in Austria formed its own singing group. Two parents and their seven children practiced their music and perfected their sound. When the unique sound was heard by others, the family was invited to sing in a festival in their home city of Salzburg.

Maybe you have seen the film *The Sound of Music.* The film is based on the story of this famous family. They were called the Trapp Family Singers.

Eventually, three more children were born, enlarging the family chorus to twelve members. The Trapps performed in concerts all over the world for twenty years, from 1939 to 1959. They shared a love of music as well as a love of family.

The Trapp family